BLOGGING

Blogging for Income

Ezekiel Brenner

© **Copyright 2018 - All rights reserved.**

In no way is it legal to reproduce, duplicate, or transmit any part of this document by either electronic means or in printed format. Recording of this publication is strictly prohibited, and any storage of this document is not allowed without written permission from the publisher.

This publication is geared towards providing exact and reliable information in regard to the topics and issues covered. The publication is not a substitute for legal, tax, financial or professional advice. If such advice is necessary, a practiced individual in the profession should be consulted.

The publisher makes no guarantees regarding income as a result of applying the information contained in this document, and any liability regarding inattention or otherwise, by any usage or abuse of any policies, processes, or directions contained within is the solitary and utter responsibility of the recipient reader, and as such, for all intents and purposes, this publication is to be considered as being "for entertainment purposes only." The reader should always seek the advice of a professional when making any legal, tax, financial, or business decisions.

Under no circumstances will any legal responsibility or blame be held against the publisher for any reparation, damages, or monetary loss due to the information herein, either directly or indirectly.

Any trademarks or brands mentioned in this publication are without any consent, permission, or backing of the trademark owner.

All trademarks and brands within this book are used only for the purposes of clarification, and are owned by the owners themselves, and not affiliated with this publication.

All copyrights not held by the publisher, are owned by the respective authors.

Introduction

My name is Ezekiel and I'm a blogger. I wasn't always a blogger though. I used to work at a job I didn't like. After work I would relieve my stress by surfing the Net. I primarily watched a lot of Youtube and read a lot of blogs. Far more than watching Youtube though, I really loved reading blogs, it was my passion, my secret pleasure that I felt most of the people around me could never quite understand.

Then I got the funny idea: "Why don't I start a blog?" And so I did.

At first I didn't know what I was doing, but there was one blogger in particular that really helped me out. He helped me so much that I would say I owe my blogging career to him. I'm not going to mention his name, because he has chosen to remain anonymous and doesn't put his real name on any of his many blogs, and neither do I for that matter. Nonetheless, I would say that I didn't do it alone, I had a mentor to look up to who showed me the ropes, so to speak. I would say mentors are very important when it comes to any pursuit, but I understand that not everyone is lucky enough to be able to find the right mentor.

This brings us to the reason I wrote this book. Like it or hate it, I wrote this book because I wanted to give people new to blogging the right guidance to put them on the right track to starting a profitable blog. This book I designed to be like a mentor, with its purpose being to get you blogging the right way, so you can avoid the common pitfalls.

However, while this book will give you a path, and has everything you need to get your blog up and running, it is not a replacement for finding a real mentor. This book in itself is a very comprehensive and complete guide to blogging, and many a blogger with a strong will has made blogging work for them without a mentor. Though I would still like to highly recommend that if you are able to find yourself a good mentor, don't pass up on that opportunity, as a good mentor will get you up to speed on things much faster than any book, though I hope you find this book to be an exceptional one. And that's all I'm going to say on the topic of mentors.

Anyway, yes this book is packed with everything you need to know to start blogging. It's going to show you the tools that you need to get in line in order to get set-up, how you should be blogging, how you should be getting your traffic, how you should be monetizing things, and much, much more! I've put everything I have into this book, so I very much hope you get something out of it.

This book assumes you have no knowledge of blogging whatsoever and holds your hand through the process of getting your blog up and getting it monetized. However, if you already have a blog, and if your only problem is the monetization aspect of things, then you will also find the answers you are looking for here.

Sometimes this book will take you out of the book to engage in some task on the Internet where further learning is required, or recommend some tool on the Internet to you, and the reason for that is that you can't learn to blog completely all in a book, and you can't start your blog in a book. I've never read a blogging book that didn't take things out of the book at one point, and that's just due to the nature of what we're learning to do, which is to create a blog which lives on the Internet, and monetize it.

In fact, there are so many aspects that go into starting a blog the right way, that separate books are actually written about each one, I'm talking about things like the basics of putting up and designing a website, learning WordPress, putting together an email marketing system, setting up your SEO (Search Engine Optimization), ways to monetize your blog, how to write magnificent blog posts, etc. Each of these aspects is a science unto themselves, so much so that some people get into just one aspect and make it their profession. For example there are web designers and developers, WordPress consultants, SEO agencies, affiliate marketing consultants, professional copywriters, and so on.

The good news is that you don't need to be a master of any of the the aforementioned aspects in order to build yourself a profitable blog, but you should be aware that they do indeed exist, and so there is always more to learn. As a newbie to blogging though, you want to focus on the main task which lies before you, which is to set up your blog and monetize it, and to only give attention to the other aspects where necessary for the purpose of improving your blog.

I don't want you to have false expectations that you're going to be a master blogger by the end of this book, as you most certainly won't be one, becoming a master of the art of blogging is a lifelong process and takes years. Even I don't consider myself a master yet; it's a constant learning process. However, I can guarantee that if you complete this book, and put time and energy into accomplishing what is taught in every lesson, then by the end of this book you will indeed be a blogger with a blog set up for monetization!

One more point before we move forward is that you should be

aware that the name I wrote this book under is not my real name, rather it is a pen name, so if you search for me and only find this book on Google, and then wonder why you can't find my blog under my name, then you know the reason why.

You might wonder why I chose to write this book under a pen name and not under the name which I use on my main blog. The reason for this is that those who read my main blog don't care one bit about learning to blog or learning to monetize a blog. It's a completely different audience in a completely different niche, so different in fact, that putting my name on a techy how-to book of how I monetized my blog would actually turn-off the audience who reads my blog. Therefore, it seemed best that if I was going to write a techy how-to book that I use a pen name, even though it might seem a little deceitful.

Yes, perhaps it is downright deceitful of me! And that's about as much as I care to confess on the topic, so let's shift our focus now to the main point of me writing this book, which is teaching you how you can implement the same strategies that I have, in order to create a profitable blog that's going to allow you to eat anything you want for the rest of your life!

Onwards to Chapter 1!

Table of Contents

Introduction	**3**
Chapter 1: Become One of Us	**8**
Chapter 2: Choosing Your Niche	**11**
Chapter 3: Starting Your Blog	**13**
Chapter 4: Creating Content	**22**
Chapter 5: Engagement and Traffic	**27**
Chapter 6: Monetizing Your Blog	**31**
Chapter 7: Email Marketing	**35**
Chapter 8: Registering with Search Engines	**42**
Chapter 9: Summing it All Up	**43**
Chapter 10: Wrapping Up	**45**

Chapter 1: Become One of Us

Bloggers are people who regularly upload written content to their websites. Each piece of uploaded content is called a blog post, and the web page that blog posts are posted to is referred to as a blog.

As long as a blogger writes blog posts, their blog will grow and they'll find more and more readers discovering their blog. If they keep up this pursuit and if their content is good, then at some point they will find that they've developed a following. If they properly set up their blog for monetization from the start, then as their following grows, so will their income. This is the theory as well as the goal!

Learning to monetize your blog can give you the opportunity to write about what you are passionate about and get paid for it. What could be better than that? This is the dream for all who endeavor to become successful at this blogging thing! Thus, for anyone who has an interest in taking up this pursuit, as your blog grows this can turn into a way to ditch your 9-to-5 and become financially free. However, if it was that easy, everyone would do it, so there are many challenges. Some of these challenges are so great that many quit at some point on the path. And so, only the most dedicated of bloggers can make it. If you're the type who starts things and easily quits when the going gets tough, then I could not recommend the path of blogging to you.

"*Blogging:* Blogging for Income" discusses everything you need to know to start a blog and monetize it so it can generate an income for you. You will be walked through all of the steps for creating a blog, generating a following, and of course monetizing it. By the end of this book, you will know everything that you need to know to enable you to create a thriving blog, as well as a paycheck. All you have to do is take action!

I know it must seem like a complete fantasy at this point, but please know that this is a very real and very valid way to earn an income. Many bloggers are doing it, and I am doing it, and if you wanted to you could by all means do it as well.

Just think about it for a moment, the Internet is growing all over the world, billions of people are getting online and many are falling in love with and discovering new blogs every day, and the main language of Internet commerce that everyone is using, for the most part, is English. Therefore, if you can write in English, and if you can regularly write blog posts in an area that you're passionate about, and if you follow this book's method for monetizing your blog, there is no reason why you can't do this as well!

How can I be so certain that this works (besides the fact that I make a living off of my blog)? Well, just take a look at all of the blogs out there that have been around for a while, you think all these people are working so hard on their blogs for free? Of course not, they're getting paid. The proof is all over the Internet, so just know that if you go into this with good intentions and keep at it, you can get paid too, and become one of us, a blogger, and hopefully at some point a financially free blogger!

If you have doubts, well right you should, because as I mentioned, it's not easy! But it is most definitely doable! And if you can write, and figure out how to point and click a mouse or use a trackpad, then this is something you can definitely do!

Chapter 2: Choosing Your Niche

Before you even think of blogging, the first thing that you have to do is choose a niche that you want to blog in.

The niche you choose should be something that you are passionate about. Not passionate about anything? Then you need to find your passion first.

Of course, you could always pick something that you are not passionate about and blog about that. However, if you do that, then you'll always be dreading writing blog posts and you'll most likely quit.

Most people who start blogging end up quitting far too early. Therefore, if you're going to be successful at blogging you're going to need to think about what you are passionate about and blog about that. It could be anything from toasting bagels to the stock market. As long as it's something that you're really into that you can write about, then you'll do just fine as a blogger.

A lot of people tend to ignore it when I say they should write about their passion and choose to write about something they kind of like. Well, I'm sorry to say this, but something you just kind of like isn't good enough! You'd better darn well be so into whatever it is that you plan to blog about that you are thinking about it all the time.

If you're going to be a student of this book, there is no approaching this blogging endeavor half-heartedly, because you're going to be putting your heart and soul into this blog in order to make it shine.

If you have no passion and just kind of like one thing or another, then your chance of success will be dismal. It won't be impossible if you put in the work, but it will just be a heck of a lot harder for you.

However, if you do have a passion, then you have a severe advantage, because the sad reality is that most bloggers don't actually feel so strongly about what they blog about. In fact, everyone who I've ever known who started a blog and was truly passionate about their niche was able to grow their blog into a success. And everyone who I've ever known who started a blog and was not really passionate about their niche failed miserably.

Therefore, the bottom line is to pick the thing that you are most passionate about and blog about that. And if you don't know what you are passionate about, then you need to start seriously thinking about it, before you even attempt to start a blog.

Chapter 3: Starting Your Blog

The first step to making money from your blog is to actually start one. If you already have a blog in place, you might still want to read through this chapter as it will provide you with the information you need to create a blog that you will be able to profit from. Aside from actually putting up a blog, you need to have several other factors in place to make sure your blog is set up for monetization.

Picking a Hosting Company

The very first step in creating a blog is choosing what hosting company you want to use. A hosting company is basically a company that owns a server that you rent space on so that you can put stuff on that space, stuff like your blog! A good hosting company will have fast servers that will allow people to be able to easily access your blog with minimal loading time.

Now, you could host your own blog, but that would require that you purchase your own server and run it 24 hours a day, which can be costly. Thus, you're best to go with a hosting company. A good hosting company is very much the backbone of your blogging business, as without a hosting company to serve your blog to the Internet, you have nothing.

Thus, I've spent hundreds of hours researching the best hosting company that a blogger can use. I am very much a cheap-skate when it comes to picking a hosting provider, and my criteria for choosing a host was to find one that would be stable, easy to use, and have the fastest loading time possible for my money.

You can do your own research and pick any host you like, or you can benefit from my hundreds of hours of research and use the same host that I use.

To find out about the host that I use, go to the following URL:

BloggerBlogger.com/

Once you're there, put your email in the form and click "Submit," and I'll then reveal to you the name of the hosting company I use, and you'll also join my blogging newsletter, though not to worry, as it's a great newsletter.

The reason that I don't mention the name of the company in this book, is because if anything ever changed, and I figured out that another hosting company was better for some reason, I might change my host. So by allowing me to email you, you will be sure to get my most updated top hosting pick.

Now, if you're thinking, "oh no, he wants me to buy something." Then let me just say that to start a blog that is yours, you're going to need hosting anyway, so yes you do have to buy hosting in any case, it's something all bloggers pay for. Don't worry though, it won't cost you an arm and a leg. I only go for the very cheapest level of hosting that ticks off all of the boxes, such as stability, speed, and ease of use. And as bloggers, that is pretty much all we need.

Sure there are many websites where you can write blog posts for free, but you won't own that webpage, and so if that site decides to make some change, they could just pull your blog away from you, or they could put ads all over your blog, or they can do just about anything they like with your blog, because it's not yours. Also, most of those websites that allow you to create a free blog do not allow you to monetize your blog in the way this book will teach you to monetize.

You want a blog that is yours completely, one that you own. Therefore, if your goal is to indeed blog for profit, you do need hosting.

Domain Name

One of the most important points of starting your blog is choosing a name. When I say a name, I mean a domain name, so it's going to be a word or group of words followed by a dot com. Still, you don't want to take it too seriously, or it could become an excruciatingly difficult ordeal that stops you from ever creating a blog. You want to choose a name that is going to reflect the topic of your blog and its personality while keeping it as short and to-the-point as possible.

At the time of this writing, the hosting company that I recommend gives you your domain for free as part of their hosting package, and I believe this will be the case for quite some time to come, as it's become an accepted standard for a hosting provider to offer at least one domain name for free when someone buys a hosting package.

Your domain name is one thing that you won't be able to change once you have chosen it. You will choose your domain name once and only once, and your entire brand and image will be built with that name attached to it. If you change your name later, you will confuse your followers and potentially lose a lot of them. Therefore, it is important that the name you choose is one that you like and one that your blog can grow along with, as well as one that is not already taken.

What you want to do is start making a list of names that you like, and you can later check the names on your list one by one at your hosting company's website to see which are taken and which are available. If the name you want is taken, then you'll have to keep thinking and searching for names until you find one that is not taken which you like.

I should also say that if you wanted to have many blogs and have many domain names, then you'd use another service called a registrar to manage your domain names. However, you need to make one blog profitable before you start going off on wild tangents buying all kinds of domain names, so we're going to focus on setting things up in a way to make it as easy as possible for you to get your first blog up, and get you to the point where you're writing blog posts on a fully monetized blog. Thus, don't worry about registering a bunch of domain names at this point, rather just focus on one.

Once you're making enough off of your first blog to pay for your hosting and living expenses, that's the point where you can consider if you'd want to start another blog, but until that point, one domain name is all you'll need, so we're not going to worry about registrars at this point. Just one blog is capable of generating hundreds, thousands, or even millions of dollars in revenue, so just one blog is probably all you will ever need.

Email

Yes, there are many free email providers out there. However, you're going to want a professional email, something that looks like: Your-Name@Your-Blog's-Name.com, and the good news is that your hosting provider will provide you with this for free. Not all hosts provide this for free, but at the time of this writing it is a standard practice of hosts to offer you professional email for free as part of their hosting package, and their support will help you to get it set up.

You can even get it set up so that you can check your email on your mobile phone, so you can easily check and reply to your email from anywhere. Or if you don't have a mobile phone, then checking it from your computer is fine for now. Though I recommend getting a mobile phone once your blog is earning enough where it can pay for one.

The fact is that you need a professional email that you own, one that you can use for communication. Since when you have a large and popular blog that's generating you an income, you'll find that you're going to need to communicate via email a lot.

Autoresponder

Apart from hosting, you're going to need an autoresponder at some point, and unfortunately this is a service that will not come with any hosting package.

The purpose of having an autoresponder is for the purpose of building an email list of your blog's followers.

We'll get into what you're going to be doing with your autoresponder in Chapter 7, but for now, just know that this is another service that you're going to need. While you could get away with starting a blog without an autoresponder, your growth is going to be very slow and you'll make much less compared to if you use an autoresponder, more on this in Chapter 7.

To find out which autoresponder I use and recommend, go to:

BloggerBlogger.com/

It's the same link I gave you to find out what I recommend for hosting, so if you already went there, then you should already know what autoresponder I recommend.

The reason I don't tell you what autoresponder I recommend in this book is also the same reason as for hosting, because I want to give you the most updated information on it.

Writing Your First Blog Post

The next important part of the process is to actually write your first blog post. In order to design your blog, you're going to have to get good at the same platform that all successful bloggers use, and that platform is called WordPress. Now there are entire books written on WordPress, and the functionality of WordPress changes with each update, so I can't recommend you read any book on it, because every book on WordPress (if not released very recently) would be teaching you something outdated.

Therefore, to make sure you have the most updated information available to you, in the same place where I keep my top hosting and autoresponder picks, I'm also going to share a link with you for a free WordPress video tutorial. I personally keep this link always updated. The tutorial will teach you everything you need to know from installing WordPress to making your first blog post.

As a blogger, you don't have to learn how to use every single feature on WordPress or become a WordPress master, rather you only need to know how to simply create and publish blog posts, which is rather simple actually.

Your hosting company will have support that will help you install WordPress and answer any WordPress related questions that you may have related to installation.

Choosing a Theme

A theme is basically how your WordPress website will look. In essence a theme is a preformatted layout possessing every design element from the colors of your blog to the fonts of the text in your headlines and blog posts.

In order to choose a theme you go to the left sidebar and hover over "Appearance" which will cause a menu to pop up. In that menu you want to then click on the word "Themes." You will then be taken to a page that shows your pre-installed themes. You then want to look for where it says "Add New Theme" and click on it. Most of the themes you'll find here are free. Take a look around and see what they've got, you can click the "Preview" button on any theme to be able to see it in greater detail. When you find one you like, click on it, then click the "Install" button, and then click the "Activate" button.

Don't worry about if you are not absolutely totally thrilled with the theme you chose, because you can always change your theme at anytime and it won't affect anything on your blog besides the look. And should it affect something, you can very easily switch back to your original theme.

Now, there is also a kind of theme that is called a premium theme. Premium themes generally aren't free, though have features that allow you to better customize your blog. I myself prefer to use premium themes, and I'll recommend to you the premium theme that I use in the same place where I recommend hosting and everything else to you.

Builder Plugin

Another pay for option you might want to consider is something called a builder plugin. There are many kinds of builder plugins, and these will allow you to forgo the whole WordPress way of designing a blog and allow you to really get in there and customize things even further. Some premium themes have builder plugins built into them, but not all of them do. I'll recommend for you the same builder plugin that I use in the same place where I recommend hosting and everything else.

Tasks to Accomplish

Before going to the next chapter, you should have accomplished the following:

1. Obtain hosting with a domain name of your choice.

2. Contact your host's support and have them walk you through setting up an email address, so you can send and receive email.

3. Obtain an autoresponder.

4. Take an online WordPress tutorial, install WordPress, and make your first blog post.

5. Choose a free Theme and activate it.

Note: Be sure to take your time and familiarize yourself with the hosting platform you choose. Also, be sure to take your time and familiarize yourself with WordPress before moving on. Most hosts these days (including the one I currently recommend as of this writing) have WordPress tutorials for you that should contain the most updated lessons on how to use WordPress, so please go through as much of their tutorials regarding WordPress as possible before moving on.

If you accomplished the steps above, then congratulations, as you'll never have to go through any of that again, and now we're ready to get into the fun stuff!

Chapter 4: Creating Content

The most important thing in your blog is the content. If people don't like the content, they are not likely to going to ever want to come back. Therefore, it's absolutely critical that you create awesome content.

Creating content that hooks people and keeps them reading is the biggest part of being a successful blogger. People should find your content so utterly mind blowing that they feel they must go through all of your posts and read everything, as well as come back and read all of your latest posts.

Let's take a more in-depth look at what a successful blog-post consists of:

Headline

The first part of making a successful blog post is to ensure that you have a killer headline. Your headline should be captivating, draw people in, and give them an idea of what you are going to be talking about in your post. It's best to take some time to really think carefully about the message your headline will convey.

You should also start reading headlines elsewhere to get ideas. Look at other blogs, magazines, and even newspaper articles and see what other headlines out there make you want to read the article. Notice which headlines grab your attention and which ones don't. The more you do this, the better you'll be able to assess what goes into a good headline, which will in turn allow you to write better headlines. For some, they'll naturally be able to do this rather quickly, for others it might take a bit of time, but as long as you make a conscious effort to analyze headlines when you see them and improve your headline writing skills, you'll become better and better at writing headlines.

Introduction Paragraph

Just like your headline, your introduction paragraph needs to be captivating and draw people in. Before anyone scrolls down to read your blog post, they are going to look at the headline and the introduction paragraph and then make a decision about whether they want to read further based on that. Thus, you need to make sure that both are going to make your readers want to keep reading.

Usually, this paragraph will be a summary of what is to come. Though a simple summary alone just won't do, it has to be captivating! Therefore, as you write your introduction paragraph, you need to consider how you're going to present things in a manner that captivates your readers. How you captivate your readers with your introduction paragraph will be different in every blog post.

Though, if you're completely lost as to how to captivate your readers with your intro paragraph, then my advice would be to write your introduction paragraph with a high degree of passion and excitement. You want to get as much passion and excitement as you can possibly get into your intro paragraph. You want is so packed full of raw passion and excitement that your readers simply can't resist reading on.

Body Paragraphs

Body paragraphs are the meat and potatoes of your blog posts, and for the most part they are your blog posts.

You want to make sure your grammar is flawless and that you are using language that will resonate well with your audience. It is here in your body paragraphs that you want to provide value. Readers don't like reading filler material, so don't include any. Readers want the real goods, and that's what you need to put here.

With each blog post, you typically want to write around 500 to 3,000 words. If you don't have enough information to create a blog post of this length that is informative and without filler, then you should either pick a different topic or do some more research on it so you have more to write about.

Sub-Headlines

Breaking up your blog post with sub-headlines will help you grab the attention of your readers. Sub-headlines should use no more than 4 words and should be clearly titled. You can use clever wording here, but the primary point is to outline what you will be talking about in your blog-post. Sub-headlines give those who like to scroll the opportunity to see what they stand to gain if they stop to read it.

If you are not quite sure about where to place sub-headlines, they should go in any section where you are focusing on a specific area within your blog post. For example, this very chapter is discussing the topic of creating content, but within this chapter is a sub-topic about sub-headlines, which is entitled "sub-headlines." You want to follow the same model with your own content in your blog posts.

In addition to giving you the opportunity to let people know what to expect, sub-headlines break up your blog posts into bite-sized bits to make it easier for readers to consume. With a generation of people who are interested in consuming things as quickly as possible, it can be hard to get people to stay focused on an entire page of words. By introducing sub-headlines, you give their eyes a brief break and provide them with an opportunity to bring their focus back.

Conclusion Paragraph

You always want to end all of your blog posts with a powerful conclusion paragraph. Your conclusion should recap exactly what your entire blog post is about, as well as make that final point that your entire post has been leading up to.

Alternative Forms of Content

Blogs are most popular for their written content, but you should be including other forms of content as well, such as images, infographics, videos, audio tracks, slideshow presentations, or anything else you can think of that you can get in there.

Many types of alternative forms of content will help you to add a more dynamic look and feel to your blog. Well placed alternative content will give people more to look at, and will make your blog more pleasing to the eye and memorable.

The most important rule to follow when using alternative content, is that it be relevant and congruent with your blog post. If it's not relevant and not congruent, don't use it, because no alternative content is better than something way out of left field that has no point being there. For example, if I was writing a blog post about cooking some great dessert, and I dropped random drawings of pink elephants in there, people wouldn't be able to take my post seriously. However, if I dropped in images of the dessert itself, it would be both relevant and congruent with my blog post. I realize this is pretty common sense stuff, but you'd be surprised at the number of blogs out there who get this part wrong.

Chapter 5: Engagement and Traffic

It is highly important that you have readers actively engage with your blog on a regular basis.

Linking to Other Blog Posts

The best way to promote engagement is to reference your other blog posts, such as writing something like "to read more about this, click the link here." The link sends readers to another blog post and keeps them on your blog. The more readers click around inside your blog the better your blog will rank in search results.

You won't be able to do this with your first blog post, since you have nothing else, but you want to get in a habit of doing this from your second blog post onwards.

Each blog post you write should bring up some topic that they can read about in more detail in another blog post. And it's even better if you can reference more than one blog post in each blog post.

Most other bloggers are not implementing this trick, but you'll find that the successful ones are.

Sharing

Having your posts shared by your readers is a great way to get in front of even more readers.

You can encourage people to share your posts by straight out asking them to somewhere within your post, such as in the conclusion paragraph. You should make your post easy to share by having sharing buttons for various social media platforms integrated as well. This makes it easy for others who enjoyed the post to effortlessly repost it to their own social media platforms. When this happens, you get yourself in front of a whole new audience, the friends of your existing audience.

In many cases, people who are into your niche know other people who are into your niche, and so they're willing to share your posts if you make it easy for them to do so.

Sharing buttons that you can add to your blog posts to make it easy for you readers to share them can be found in both the theme or page builder I recommend at:

BloggerBlogger.com/

Or if you don't want the theme or page builder I recommend, there is a free plugin that as of this writing comes pre-installed on your WordPress called Jetpack that also has sharing buttons which you could use. I find it easiest to use the ones that come with my theme, but there are multiple ways to get sharing buttons working.

Social Media Platforms

Social media is a perfect place to get the word out about your blog.

You want to make a Facebook Page about your blog, and each

time you write a new blog post you want to post an image to your Facebook page that links to the respective blog post. Likewise, you also want to create a Twitter account for your blog and tweet a link of each new blog post you publish.

Also, you might want to consider creating a free Facebook Group for your niche, managed by your Facebook Page, and make sure you pin a post to the top of your Facebook Group that has a link going directly to your blog.

If you like making videos, Youtube is also a great place to get traffic to your blog from, by posting a video each time you make a blog post with a link in the description of each video going to the associated blog post.

Now, each of these social media platforms, Facebook, Twitter, and Youtube are sciences unto themselves, but it's worth learning how to use each, since each of them can serve as a great source of traffic to your blog.

Other social media platforms you might want to consider getting into are Instagram, Pinterest, LinkedIn, and Reddit.

Since learning all of these social media platforms can be daunting. I would recommend at first just starting out with one. Focus on getting traffic from just one, and when you feel your squeezing that one out of just about all of the traffic it's going to produce for you on a regular basis, then that's when it's time to choose another one.

The Bottom Line

The bottom line is that the more readers are clicking around within your blog, and the more new readers click over to your blog from social media platforms, the higher the chance that you'll retain some of those readers as long-term followers, and also the higher your blog will rank better in search engines as a result of all of the click-happy traffic you're getting.

Chapter 6: Monetizing Your Blog

Your Own Product

The first way you should be monetizing your blog is with your own product, if you have one. If not, then no problem, as there are other ways to monetize your blog without having your own product that we're going to get into in this chapter.

If you don't have a product though, you should think about creating one. Your product could be anything from an ebook to a video course to some cool item that you make yourself in your garage. It's really your call what product you want to sell.

For most new blogs, creating a niche related ebook that your readers would be interested in purchasing would be the way to go at first, until you come up with another product idea.

If your product is an ebook, the easiest way to sell this from your blog would be to upload it to Amazon's KDP platform, which can be found at:

kdp.amazon.com

And then put a link to your ebook on your blog. The benefit of using a service like Amazon for your ebook is that you can also make sales from Amazon shoppers who might stumble upon your ebook when searching the Amazon store. Based on that, it's a good idea to make sure that you put a link to your blog in your ebook, so that anyone who hasn't heard of your blog who buys the ebook could easily click your link to find your blog and potentially become a follower.

Affiliate Products

The reality is, that you really don't need your own product. Many bloggers who earn an utter fortune blogging do it entirely by promoting affiliate products.

In case you don't know what an affiliate product is, allow me to brief you on the matter. An affiliate product is the product of another company that you put on your website, and when someone clicks on the link of that product and buys it, you get paid a percentage of the profits.

In order to promote affiliate products, you need to first of all join affiliate programs of companies that have affiliate products related to your niche. If your niche was meditation for example, you would simply type in your Google search bar "meditation affiliate," and all affiliate programs related to meditation will pop up.

There are so many affiliate programs out there for almost every niche that you're bound to find something no matter what your niche is. Even Amazon has an affiliate program which can be found at:

affiliate-program.amazon.com

Just enrolling in Amazon's affiliate program alone will allow you to promote any product they have on their store.

Once you find an affiliate program that matches your needs, you simply want to register for it. For most affiliate programs this means filling out a form with your information, such as name and address, and also your bank information so they can pay you.

Once you register with an affiliate program, you'll then be given access to an affiliate dashboard where you can get affiliate links and banners. These affiliate links and banners are what you would put on your blog. If someone were to click on them and make a purchase, you would make money.

Now, you don't want to go wild and promote every affiliate product out there. You want to choose a handful of products that you are confident about that you can keep promoting, maybe around 3 to 5 affiliate products. And you want to put the affiliate banners to these products in your blog's sidebar and in your blog's footer.

You can put them in your blog's sidebar and footer by going to your WordPress dashboard and going to that big column on the left side, and hovering over Appearance which will cause a menu to pop up, and then you click on Widgets in that menu. This will take you to the Widgets page.

In the Widgets page, you will basically look for a block-like thing that says Sidebar, and multiple block-like things that say Footer Area. You should find these on the right side if the Widgets page.

On the left side of the page, you should see an Available Widgets section. What you want to do now is find a Text widget and then click on it and drag it to either the Sidebar block-like thing on the right, or on one of the Footer Area block-like things, and then release. It should stick there if you did it correctly.

Next you want to open the Text widget, and fill in a title for it and below the Title you'll see 2 tabs, one called Visual and one called Text. You want to click on the Text tab, and this is where you'll paste in your banner code for your affiliate banner. Then you click the blue Save button below where you just pasted the code.

If you did it right, then when you look at your blog now, you'll see your affiliate banner there. This means you're set up to get paid.

I would recommend putting the same affiliate banners in both your sidebar and footer. Though it's up to you how you would like to do it. As long as they are there and are visible, then your blog is monetized from an affiliate banner perspective.

One last thing I should mention, the FTC has some regulations about disclosing affiliate links, and you need to follow them. You can find a link to information about disclosing affiliate links on the FTC's website at:

BloggerBlogger.com/

Now, I've never heard of a blogger ever being busted by the FTC for failing to disclose, but you don't want to be the first that it happens to, so I'd recommend you take some time and read about the FTC's guidelines about it to make sure you understand them.

Email Marketing

Another way to monetize your blog, and to ensure that it has a high retention rate is to create an email list of your followers, and that's exactly what we'll be covering how to do in the next chapter.

Chapter 7: Email Marketing

Autoresponder Service

In order to engage in email marketing, you first of all have to learn how you should set things up in order to build a list, and in order to do that you're going to need an autoresponder service.

I know what you're thinking. You're thinking: "Oh no! Another thing I need to pay for!"

And you would be correct. Now there are free services out there, but I haven't found any of those free services to be reliable. I mean you're going to need to build a huge list of your followers, and if something goes wrong and your data gets lost, do you really think a free service is going to do very much to help you retrieve your lost list?

The other issue with free services is that most of those do not allow you to market affiliate products to your list, and if you do it and get caught, they'll cancel your account and then just snatch your list away from you.

You want to think of an autoresponder as being like a cell phone. It is your communication line to your followers. You want to be able to just shoot out one email and have it reach all of your followers, and that's what an autoresponder service is good for.

Let's be clear on the points on why you should be using an autoresponder to build an email list:
1. It will increase your blog's retention rate, because you'll be able to notify your readers when you publish new blog posts.
2. You want to send affiliate offers to your list.
3. You want to be able to tell your list when you release a new product.

If you've never dealt with an autoresponder before, then I'd like to make it clear that some email service like Gmail or Yahoo will simply not work. You need something with more power than that. As mentioned, you need the ability to shoot out one email and have it reach your thousands or tens of thousands of followers all in one go.

To find out my pick for an autoresponder if you didn't already see it, just go to:

BloggerBlogger.com/

How to Build a List

In a nutshell, what you want to do is put a form provided by your autoresponder service on your blog, and offer a newsletter plus something of value to anyone who signs up for your list. The something of value is called a lead magnet. The lead magnet will usually be a mini-book or report related to your niche or a video teaching how to do something, and it should be attached to the first email someone gets upon subscribing to your list. If it's not attached to your first email, there should be a link in your first email that goes to the lead magnet.

You're essentially trading the lead magnet for signups to your newsletter. Sure, you don't have to offer a lead magnet and can have the newsletter itself be the thing of value. Though I have tried it both ways, and what I've found is that you'll grow a list much faster if you offer a lead magnet; and not only I have figured this out, because all of the top bloggers are doing it. Why are myself and all of the top bloggers doing it? Well, obviously because it just plainly works!

Your autoresponder's customer support will walk you through how to get the form set up on your website (that's their job) and will even have tutorials for you on how to set this up, so no point for me to teach you how to use an autoresponder service, since they'll be able to teach you how to use their service better than me. After all, that's what you're paying for when you join an autoresponder service.

You'll have no problems growing your email list once you get that set up correctly.

How to Create a Lead Magnet

The best way to create a lead magnet is to think about something small that would be easy to create that your audience will find valuable and to create it.

For example, let's say your blog is about Tennis. Then something that would make a good lead magnet might be a report covering your picks for the top 5 tennis rackets, since this is something that anyone into tennis or anyone looking to get into tennis would find valuable. You even could (and should) put affiliate links to all 5 of the tennis rackets in your report, so that you'd get paid if someone clicks the link in your report to any one of the rackets and makes a purchase.

To create such a report, you would open up your word processing software (whether MS Word, Apple Pages, or Google Docs, whichever one you use is fine), and simply write it, and try to put in some images in there, and of course links (affiliate links would be best). Once you feel it looks good, then simply export what you wrote to a PDF file.

That PDF file is your lead magnet.

Now, I'm guessing that people into tennis would be willing to trade their email addresses for a lead magnet like that, and that they would find such a lead magnet valuable.

A lead magnet doesn't need to be complex or be something that takes you weeks to create. Rather it should be something of a good enough level of value that someone would simply be willing to give you their email address in exchange for it. That said, it should be high quality and look as professional as you can get it to look.

To know what kind of lead magnet your audience would be willing to trade their email for, you have to basically put yourself in their shoes and ask yourself what you would be willing to trade your email address for.

Now, if you find that you're not able to grow a large email list off of your lead magnet, then you have to think about whether it's because it wasn't a good lead magnet, or is it because your blog is not getting enough traffic yet.

Though some people will join your list just to get your lead magnet and then immediately unsubscribe from your list. Not to worry when this happens though, as it's just a normal part of the game, it happens to all of us. Though most who subscribe to your list will likely stick around, especially if they are actually into your niche, because they're hoping to get more value from you.

What to Email Your List

Once you've got a growing list, you need to email them, and you need to email them regularly. Otherwise your list may become cold and you'll get a lot of people unsubscribing, because they didn't join your list just for your lead magnet. They joined it because they expect a newsletter from you as well, a newsletter with, you guessed it, some kind of value of course.

Basically though, you want to email your list about 2 or 3 times a week. You should be emailing them to inform them about an amazing new blog post that you've just published. Now, if you're publishing blog posts every day, then don't email them every day or they may get annoyed and unsubscribe, rather just email them about the good ones, and try to sell them on clicking your link to check out your latest posts.

You should also be emailing them some valuable content that they won't find in your blog, some newsletterly like content. If you have trouble coming up with newsletterly like content, then I'd recommend you find some blogs and join other blogger's email lists and see what they email you. The things that you liked that they emailed you, you should note down to think about later. When later comes, you should be thinking: Why did you like those certain emails? And then try to incorporate the things you like into your own newsletter.

Don't worry if some people unsubscribe from your list every time you send an email. This is normal and part of the game, don't take it personally. People have different reasons for unsubscribing, and so you should just assume that they had their reasons.

Lastly, every now and then you want to email your list an affiliate offer relevant to something you write them in your newsletter. And if you do a good job providing value to your list, you'll get some buyers, and you'll make some money this way.

In fact, most bloggers who are successful get so good at emailing their list that they make the majority of their income from their list. Thus, the list is actually the most important thing, and sending out a regular newsletter to them is a critical part of your blogging business!

Yes, your blog is an entity within itself that can be profitable on its own, but it should also serve as a means by which to get people onto your email list.

I mean, let's face it, receiving an email is more personal than reading a blog post.

Sure you'll make some money just off of having affiliate banners on your blog, but that is nothing compared to what you'll make with an email list! Consider the banners on your blog as something that will provide a little bit of income here and there, though as your blog grows, that traffic will increase and you'll make even more from those banners. Though still, it's a small drop in the bucket compared to what you'll make from your list!

The Big Secret

You see, here is the big secret to monetizing a blog: And the secret is, drumroll please… The list is everything!

Bloggers who blog for years and wonder why they can't make any money are not doing so simply because they haven't built an email list.

You see, you need to think of your blog as a gateway, a gateway to your list. Your gateway should look pretty and provide a ton of value, but the real magic should be happening when you email your list.

You see, these people on your list are there because they see you as the authority on your topic and they want news from you, updates, and they expect you to keep them connected to the scene of whatever your niche is. They always want to hear about products you recommend, and they are also interested in your products as well (if you've created any).

I know what you're thinking, you're thinking: Well, I already have a handful of affiliate banners on my blog, and some more affiliate links in my lead magnet, so what kinds of affiliate offers am I supposed to be emailing people on my list and where do I get them?

And if you're thinking that, then you're thinking the right way!

You need to make it your mission to register with every affiliate program for any kind of product that your followers might be interested in. However, they should be high quality products. And you need to send your list offers for those products. Maybe 2 to 4 offers a month or it could be more. You don't actually need to have tried all of those products yourself (though it's better if you have tried them). If you didn't try a product, there is no need to lie, you can just tell your list that you heard good things about it and were thinking about trying it, and leave an affiliate link to it of course.

At the same time, you should now and then talk about the products on the banners of your blog, and tell your list about the ins and outs of those products (providing more value), and leave affiliate links to them in your emails when you talk about them.

Eventually, you want to create your own products, that you can also sell to your list. Your product could be an ebook, or something else, it can be anything your list would be interested in that you can create.

Emailing a list is not easy, but the whole point of your blog is to actually grow your list, because that's where the real money is at!

If you have any doubts on how you should be emailing your list, then (as previously mentioned) make sure you subscribe to the email lists of other bloggers to see how they do it.

Chapter 8: Registering with Search Engines

Register Your Site With Google

To get traffic, the first thing you want to do is register your site with Google.

To register your site with Google, it's best to follow Google's instructions on it, since they are the authorities on the matter. You can find the link to Google's instructions on how to do that directly at, you guessed It:

BloggerBlogger.com/

Other than registering with Google, you might also want to register with Bing. And you can find that link at the same place.

Yes, I've set up everything for you at the same link.

Once you're registered with both of those, that's pretty much all you need to do, since these days Google and Bing are pretty much it as far as search engines go.

Chapter 9: Summing it All Up

To sum it all up.

You need to get hosting and an autoresponder.

You need to choose a Theme and start writing blog posts, one a day if you can! Or as many as you can do in a week.

You need to get on social media and get out the word about your blog.

You need to get affiliate banners on your blog in your sidebar and footer.

You need to create a lead magnet.

You need to set up a form on your blog for capturing email addresses to add to your list.

You need to set things up with your autoresponder so it emails your subscribers your lead magnet when they sign up at your form.

You need to email your list regularly.

If you have all of that set up. Then all you're doing now is writing blog posts, emailing your list, and doing social media to keep trying to get new traffic over to your blog. And if that's the point where you're at, then you're doing well.

As long as you keep doing that (posting, emailing, social media) your blog will continue to grow, and at some point you'll start to see money come in. Now it could take weeks, or it could take months, rarely does it ever take more than a year. Just keep going and trying to improve all aspects of your blog as time passes.

Keep trying to get better with WordPress.

Keep trying to get better with your Autoresponder.

And keep learning, the learning process never stops!

If you keep on it, eventually you'll hit a point where your blog turns into a profit machine.

However, don't stop there, keep going, keep improving.

Chapter 10: Wrapping Up

Well, we've covered a lot, and I hope you got a lot out of this book.

I know it's difficult to wrap one's head over the many concepts laid out here, but feel free to reread things over if you need to, however many times you need to, and this should all click at some point.

Armed with what you've learned here, I know you're going to do just fine at monetizing your blog and making it work for you. In fact, I'm sure of it, because these strategies just simply work! And are exactly what it takes to monetize a blog.

I wish you the best of success in your blogging endeavor!

I've given you the entire secret to my success as a blogger.

You have the knowledge, now all you need to do is take action!

Also, if you have a spare moment, please do go ahead and leave a review for this book.

And when you're a big success, please don't hesitate to shoot me a message and let me know all about your success story.

I know you're going to do just fine!

Thank you for taking the time to read this book.

Let's get blogging now!

www.ingramcontent.com/pod-product-compliance
Lightning Source LLC
Chambersburg PA
CBHW070139230526
45472CB00004B/1606